Understanding God's Commandments in Today's World

Prophetess Joyce Chapman

ISBN: 979-8-88615-360-6 (Paperback)
979-8-88615-361-3 (Hardback)
979-8-88615-362-0 (Ebook)

Inks and Bindings
888-290-5218
www.inksandbindings.com
orders@inksandbindings.com

EXODUS 20: 1-27

And God spoke all these words, saying

I am the Lord they God, which have brought thee out of the land of

Egypt, and of the house of bondage

Thou shalt have no other gods before me

Thou shalt not make unto thee any graven image, or any likeness of anything that is in heaven above, or

what is in the earth, or that is in the water under earth:

Thou shalt not bow down thyself to them, nor serve them: for

I the Lord am a jealous God, visiting the iniquity of the fathers upon the children unto the third and

fourth generation of them that hate me:

And shewing mercy unto thousands of them that love me, and keep my commandments

Thou shalt not take the name of the Lord thy God in vain; for the Lord will not hold him guiltless that

taketh his name in vain,

Remember the Sabbath day, to keep it holy

Six days shalt thou labour, and do all thy work;

But the seventh day is the Sabbath of the Lord thy God: in it thou shalt not do any work, thou, nor thy

son, nor thy daughter, thy manservant, nor thy maidservant, nor thy cattle, nor thy stranger that is

within thy gates:

For in six days the Lord made heaven and earth, the sea: wherefore the Lord blessed the Sabbath day,

and hallowed it

Honor thy father and thy mother: that thy days may be long upon the land which the Lord thy God

giveth thee

Thou shalt not kill

Thou shalt not commit adultery

Thou shalt not steal

Thou shalt not bear false witness against neighbor

Thou shalt not covet thy neighbor's house, thou shalt not cover thy neighbor's wife, nor his manservant,

nor his maidservant nor his ox, nor his ass, nor anything that is thy neighbor's

ACKNOWLEDGEMENTS

*This tribute unto **"MOST HIGH GOD" UNDERSTANDING GOD'S COMMANDMENT IN TODAYS WORLD"** came about as a direct result of encouragement and assistance from Prophetess Sharon Middleton of Woodbridge, VA, Prophetess/Pastor Bessie O'Dino of Jersey City, N.J., Bishop and Lady George Herring of Rockhill, S.C. and Elder Levi Quattlebaum of Los Angeles, CA.*

*The many years of traveling on the field of God/Elohim/Yahshua the Messiah/Jesus the Christ and being taught by the Saints of God, as I have listed Above has given myself the strength, wisdom and knowledge to carry through God/Elohim/Yahshua the Messiah/Jesus the Christ will in writing this tribute to the **"OMNIPOTENT ONE."***

ACKNOWLEDGEMENTS

The Ten Commandments of God define sin:

This book of God's/Elohim/Yahshua the Messiah Ten Commandment is dedicated to the "Most High God" that I served for the thorough and breakdown of understanding of the commandments as a blue print for living in today's world; they are equal to our guidelines for our daily living. We allow people, places and things to become our gods such as money, fame, work, pleasure and human mankind because we concentrate too much on them for meaning of security and dollar worth. We have replaced these things in place of God.

As quite as it is kept, the amount of time we occupy these things in our lives, they can grow into gods, thereby controlling our thoughts and energies. Placing God in our lives, as #1, eliminates these things from turning into God.

For further explanation:

These laws given by God/Elohim written with His own finger Ex. 31:18, Deut. 5:22, 20:2-4 and these laws were originated from the "Great I Am" and from "His" eternal character; therefore, there moral values; they cannot change and will not change. Mal 3:6.

God/Elohim Commandment were placed inside of the Ark of the Covent Deut. 10:1-15, the law of Moses was placed in the Side of the Covent Deut. 31:9,24-26.

The great things of God's law is, the principle of justice, mercy and love therein set forth man declare that the law of God/Elohim has been done away with, that the Bible is not authentic as a result, a tide of evil has come over the land.

Our God/Elohim is a God of mercy. The end of God's forbearance with those who persist in disobedience is approaching rapidly Now let's question ourselves: Ought man be surprised when punishment follows:

Transgression: Ought man be surprised when God/Elohim bring destruction and death upon those who are disobedient. The forbearance of "Yashua the Messiah" has been great, so intense when we consider the continuous insult to "His" holy commandments we marvel as evildoers!

The "Omnipotent One" has increasing power over "His" own character. But "His" will surely arise to punish the wicked, who boldly defy the just claim of "His" holy commandments.

The "Great I Am" message for the people of today is: the conditions that are prevailing in our society, proclaiming in thunder tones, the hour of "His" judgement is come and the end of all things, earthly are at hand. In quick succession the judgement's of God/Elohim will follow one another fire, flood and earthquakes coupled with war and bloodshed. Let's not be surprised by events both great and decisive; for the angel of mercy cannot remain much longer to shelter the impenitent.

God/Elohim has chosen "His" prophets to be the enforcer of "His" commandments and they (they commandments) sometimes are referred to as the "His Royal Law or Moral Law" in Greek as the "Decalog"

The storm of the "Lord Jesus Christ" wrath is gathering and only those will continue to stand who will respond to the invitation of mercy and become sanctified through obedience to the laws of the "Divine Ruler" "THE TEN COMMANDMENTS OF GOD"

FIRST COMMANDMENT

"Thou shall have no other gods before me"

Human Mankind/People: Our children, our husband/wives, our pastors/ministers, our work bosses and acquaintances/friends

Places: Our houses, (man made treasures in our homes)
Placing our children above God/Elohim, setting them apart from rules and regulations of this world and values have been depleted from the rearing of our children

Placing before our God/Elohim, our business, our pleasures, and our own ways Isaiah 58:13 such as: Children are now defiant disregard for respect criminal's element (records) boot camps and homes for those involved in negative conduct

The unsaved in ungodly business, perpetrating sexual relationships with anyone or anybody

Our own stubborn naughty and sinful ways

Disrespect for God's Holy Sabbath Day

Placing things before God/Elohim, our vehicles, our homes, our clothes (everyday necessaries) (money) dollar worth and our children

We have replaced these things in the place of God/Elohim!

In the Old Testament (the Ten Commandments) were written on tablets of stone with God's/Elohim's own finger;

In the New Testament, the same commandments are written in the hearts of man

The belief that is acceptable to God/Elohim is an active belief, a belief motivated by putting God/Elohim first: such faith begins with the First Commandment

"You shall have no other God before me"!!!

SECOND COMMANDMENT

"Thou shall not make unto thee any graven images or any likeness of anything that is in heaven above, or that is in the earth beneath, or that is in the water under the earth for the Lord thy God am a jealous God, visiting the iniquity of the Fathers upon the children unto the third and fourth generations of them that hate me: and showing mercy unto thousands of them that love me and keep my commandments"

We are to exclude any religious images, any religious statues, religious toys, any religious cards with pictures depicting God/Elohim/Yahshua the Messiah/Jesus the Christ or anything that is relevant to these things shall not be bowed to, for they are not of God. Believing in God/Elohim is not the same as loving God. And one who does not have God/Elohim does not put God/Elohim *first!*

For generations and generations to come: these idols/graven images are not to be worshipped. The only true "Yahshua the Messiah/Jesus Christ" is to be worshipped in spirit and truth St. John 4:24

We serve a God who wants to be first in our lives and who is going to be #1 in our lives to be worshipped in spirit and truth

Idolatry still exists in today's world; worshipping the flesh still is in existence Gen. 5:19-20 Like any sin, the outward expression reflects the condition of the heart Even false concepts of God/Elohim can be idolatries

The Commandments of God in the "New Testament" are found in the Book of Matthew 19:18, 20

THIRD COMMANDMENT

"Thou shalt not take the name of the Lord thy God in vain; for the Lord will not hold him guiltless that taketh his name in vain"

Is God/Elohim first in your life? Does he com before anything else?

This commandment deals with "His" name. "His" position as the great "Sovereign Ruler" of this universe.

To use it frivolously or in a common or curse is very common today, however the world fails to realize how serious it is. We must respect and use "His" name appropriately, speaking it is praise/worship, not in common tone, like people of the world for the "Saints of God" addresses this name with vigor

The world uses "His" name loosely and or in a very commonly verbalized in a profane manner

This commandment gives us direction to praise and honor the "Most High" in our thoughts, our spirit and our actions

This commandment forbids us to invoke, God/Elohim names with falsehood, therefore it condemns swearing falsely. God/Elohim name is abused through false oaths and through vulgar use of "His" names, truthful oaths, proper respect for God/Elohim encourages truthfulness, especially when you "Fear Him"

Let your "yes be yes" and your "no be no" in order that you may not fall under condemnation. The Messiah is calling the "Faithful and True" Rom. 19:11

When a person describes himself/herself as a "Saint of God" but does not live accordingly, he dishonors the name, by which he is called. Those who claim the "Messiah" as their Savior, but are seen abusing alcohol or known for immoral behavior can cause those who are not saved to speak negatively of the name of the "Messiah" For this reason an overseer, elder or pastor must be above reproach 1 Tim 3:2

FOURTH COMMANDMENT

"Remember the Sabbath Day, to keep it holy Six days shalt thou labor, and do all thy work: But the seventh day is the Sabbath of the Lord thy God: in it shalt not do any work, thou , nor thy son, nor thy daughter, thy manservant, nor thy maidservant, nor thy stranger that is within thy gates: For in six days the Lord made heaven and earth, the sea, and all that in them is, and rested the seventh day: wherefore the Lord bless the Sabbath day, and hollowed it"

This is the commandment that requires obedience and is a powerful factor in bringing the lives of men and women close to the Creator, God/Elohim, "His" blessings and direct guidance "If you love me, keep my commandment" St. John 14:15

What can be more moral, than a Sabbath of holy worship, which provides further instructions on how we are to worship "Him"

All our time belongs to God/Elohim He created the seventh day week and commanded we devote one day —the seventh day —of every week as a day of rest in "Him" and time for special worship on this day The 7th day is a Sabbath of solemn rest in "Him" a holy convocation on which "no work" is to be done Lev. 23:13, Ex. 20:9,10, Deut. 5:13-24 This is a divinely appointed time for God's/Elohim's people to assemble in worship, sing praises and offer thanks to "Him" and build one another up in faith, love and hope Keeping the Sabbath is a sign between God/Elohim and you throughout your generations It is not a god who delivered Israel from bondage, it was the God, the one and only true God Maker of the heaven and the earth — who redeemed the people and made them "His" special people The 4th commandment completes the first section of the commandments which is a perpetual observance of a sign of the relationship between God/Elohim and man

This test commandment is in its fullness the longest of any of the ten and placed protectively; as it were in the very midst of the Commandments

Who made the Sabbath? God/Elohim created the Sabbath for mankind A day of only "Him" our talk, actions and our thoughts The Sabbath Day is a consecrated time where we can completely forget our daily routine and draw closer to our God/Elohim in study, mediation, and prayer Let's go further, we know this is the best commandment "whether or not we will be true to God/Elohim" and coupled among with this day of rest in "Him" many says: see it, this is proof the Sabbath is for the Jews only The keeping of the seven day Sabbath is not just a "Jewish thing = equal for all men" According to the Scriptures Mark 2:27 The Sabbath was made for man, and not man for the Sabbath

The 4th Commandment is for all who desire to lead and want a "holy life" Isaiah 35:8 And a main road will go through that once — deserted land; it will be named "the Highway of Holiness" No evil hearted men may walk up it God will walk there with you; even the most stupid cannot miss the way

The Word (the Commandments) of God makes us know; all who live "holy unto the Most-High" will have eternal life, but are you willing in today's world of tradition (people, places, and things) to live a "holy life" before our "Father" by following/living the "Commandments of God"

As "His — Holy Sabbath Day is reflected in our instructions from "Him" for this time "He wants us to reverence Him, worship Him, and come into Holy Convocation unto Him" Isaiah 58:13,14

These instructions are not very hard to follow since "He" is our spiritual father and we want to obey our father!!!

In timing of the aspect of "What time is the Sabbath? In accordance with the Sacred calendar (Hebrew) the 7th day is/begins at evening, going down of the sun or sunset (This is God's/Elohim's time) this time differs from the Georgian calendar (Roman-man) which depicts Sunday as the (7) seventh day of the week The

Sacred calendar was established by God/Elohim and utilized by the Israelites/Jews The Georgian calendar was established by the "Gentiles" Would you not rather obey God/Elohim than man?" It is stated in Acts 5:29 Then Peter and the other apostles answered and said, we ought to obey God rather than man We must obey God's/Elohim as stated in the New Testament James 2:10 I quote: For whosoever shall keep the whole law (10 commandments) and yet offend in one point, he is guilty of all (10 commandments)

There is nothing carnal about keeping the commandments It takes a spiritual being to keep spiritual things The commandments are spiritual, holy just and good We do not make void the law by believing or having faith, we established the law even the more because, we are saved Romans 3:20,31:6:1. 15, 18:7:7,8,10

St. John 14:15 "If you love me, keep my commandments

FIFTH COMMANDMENT

"Honor thy Father and thy Mother, that thy days may be long upon the land which the Lord thy God giveth thee"

The right time to begin the path is in childhood with the help of loving God, fearing God and obeying your parents

This is the first commandment of promise: God/Elohim character is characterized chiefly by "His" grace and faithfulness to us ("His promises")

A solemn pledge to perform or grant a specific/specified thing:

All of (us) natural beings have a mother and father: We should hole them in high esteem, respect them (no matter what the circumstances are) they are due: the love and respect from us; because our God/Elohim gave them to us "He" has commanded us to honor them God/Elohim has promised us, if we honor them "He" promised to give us (the sones and daughters) more time here on earth; that our days may be longer If children return from sins of their fathers and select to love God/Elohim and keep "His Commandments: they shall reap the benefits from God

If the nation of Israel reaped the blessings of obedience to God's Covenant, they should would keep God's Commandments from generation to generation. Then it would have been impossible to dishonor, disrespect our parents in the home Our God does require the parents to teach our children "His" commandments; if we are the saved nation (House of Israel) There can be disciplinary measures guided by love, not anger

This commandment is necessary for family stability and is the foundation and of a stable society: it is a sin to dishonor parents today and forever!!!

SIXTH COMMANDMENT

"Thou shalt not kill"

This time we keep the true knowledge of "Him" amid the thunder and lightning, shaping of Mt. Sinai, God/Elohim's voice thundered though shalt not murder=kill

The taking of life, harboring hare and anger in our hearts, God/Elohim only has the wisdom and justice for all concern and only "He" has the right to take vengeance on human being, to the extent of executing them if need be. Saints of God must know that God/Elohim is real and "His" protection and "His" vengeance are just as real

We can murder/kill with our tongues, thoughts and dees: gossiping to the will of death through the tongue, in our thoughts, thinking or wishing bad things about people and what we could do to them and easily our deeds, such as the taking of life ex. abortion=the taking of one's life through our deeds (reputation, back biting and tale bearing)

SEVENTH COMMANDMENT

"Thou shalt not commit adultery"

God/Elohim gave this commandment to protect the honor and sanctity of marriage. The spirit makes very evident the fact that all unclean conduct before marriage is wrong. Due to the future, and unfaithfulness before marriage is violating the command as much as adultery committed after marriage. This marriage in God's/Elohim's sight is such a precious righteous, holy thing, that is must not be defiled! So, the first and primary purpose of marriage is to make man and woman complete. "It is not good that man should be alone; I will make a help meet for him Gen. 2:18 God/Elohim saw that man was incomplete by himself. Each is incomplete without the other.

The purpose of sex and marriage: the birthing and the training of their children. "And God blessed them, and God said until the," "Be fruitful and multiply, and replenish the earth, and subdue it" Gen. 1:28

The home and family are the basis of all decent society!

A third purpose in sex and marriage is the building of character in the home and family relationship; As ordained by God/Elohim, the marriage union is a holy thing, it is so holy that in "His Word" Almighty God uses the marriage union as a type of the relationship between Christ and His church Eph. 5:22-24. He that loveth his wife, loveth himself. Eph. 5:25-28 A godly man is to be head of his house; he gives protection, guidance and happiness to his wife and family. The Almighty God holds him responsible for being the right kind of head! "For this cause shall a man leave his father and mother, and shall be joined unto his wife, and they two shall be one flesh. Eph. 5:31 In a marriage union, man and woman are made as one. Therefore, nothing should come between them; eternal faithfulness to "Yahshua the Messiah" as our head, just as our husbands are in our family's life.

It is a reproach to Almighty God/Elohim for us to deny "His" wisdom in ordaining the marriage union; in making us truly "one flesh" with our mate! How can we be faithful to God/Elohim without being faithful to our mate?

The teaching of "Yahshua the Messiah" Whosoever shall put away his wife, except it be for fornication, and shall marry another commiteth adultery and whosoever marrieth her which is put away doth commit adultery. Matt. 19:9

God/Elohim permits divorces in certain instances "Yahshua the Messiah" exception clause "except it be for fornication" Matt. 19:9

Should be employed only as a last resort and even then, after much prayer, counsel and sincere attempts to save the marriage. And the same would apply to Apostle Paul's permission for the "Saith of God" to remarry, if deserted by an uncoveted mate. 1ˢᵗ Corinthians 7:15

Every form of adultery is so very wrong and evil because marriage is so holy and sacred in the sigh of Almighty God/Elohim.

This is an offense against God/Elohim, "Himself" and against an institution which "He" has ordained!

Modern society is paying a terrible penalty for these wide spread sins and abominations. The illicit sexual intercourse before marriage called "fornication" by God/Elohim is becoming epidemic among young people in our world of today.

"Saints of God" must make every effort to "abstain from the passion of the flesh" 1ˢᵗ Peter 2:11. Dearly beloved, I beseech you as strangers, and pilgrims, abstain from fleshly lusts, which was against the soul 2ⁿᵈ Corinthians 10:5.

Casting down imaginations, and every high thing that exaleth against the knowledge of God/Elohim and bringing into captivity every thought to the obedience of the "Messiah".

EIGHTH COMMANDMENT

"Thou shalt not steal"

This law protects the most sacred human relationships, the home, the family, and human life itself. But we violate this commandment in hundred of ways through a watered-down system of morality. For God's/ Elohim laws are living, active things — like the law of gravity. When you transgress them, the punishment is automatic and is surely going to happen.

Stealing from God/Elohim in Mal. 3:8 Will a man rob God? Yet ye have robbed me. But ye say, wherein have we robbed thee: In tithes and offering (verse 8) God/Elohim continues: Ye are cursed with a curse: for ye have robbed me even this whole nation. Then God/Elohim promises in "His Word" "Brining ye all the tithes into the storehouse, that there maybe meat in mine house, and prove me now herewith, saith the Lord of hosts: if I will not open you the windows of heaven, and pour you out a blessing, that these shall not be room enough to receive it" (verses 9-10 "He" commands this always trust in "Him". You must obey and exercise faith for time to come. But as you serve "Him", obey and trust only "Him", God will keep "His" part of the bargain, your blessings continue to unfold.

Stealing arises from the sinful condition of the heart. For out of the heart says Yahshua: evil thoughts, murder, adultery, sexual immorality are perpetrated through this sinful nature properties and possessions are to be gained by honest work. In the spirit of God/Elohim's laws, a man not only steals by taking from another, that which not his, but by refusal to work in order to share that which is his, but by refusal to work in order to share and give to others in need! "It is more blessed to give than to receive" Acts 20:35.

This law emphasizes the importance of getting all your own through lawful channels.

Give freely, not grudgingly, adding as God/Elohim says: for this the Lord your God will bless you in all your work and in all that you understand.

NINTH COMMANDMENT

"Thou shalt not bear false witness against thy neighbor"

The double standard of morality is to tell a lie!

In seeking and bearing witness to the truth is associated with God/Elohim = God is truth, as I am the way the truth and the life. John 14:6. We must learn to live and speak truthfully, if we are clean spiritually, we can speak and live truthfully; but we are living in a time of untruth, hypocrisy and self-deception. There is no more despicable sin than that of slander, the lies invented and spread abroad with intent to harm one's fellowman. But a false witness who slanders may rob one of esteem and reputation in the eyes of his fellowman. In the book of Proverbs 6:19, a false witness who breathes out lies, and one who sows discord among the brethren, God hates Truth is absolutely, necessary to godliness. Human beings bear the image of God/Elohim and are entitled to truth. A liar, therefore, disregards the dignity of others, put another way, lying is dehumanizing Satan lies, he speaks out of his own character and is the father of lies, John 8:44. His servants (Satan) masters of deceptions, disguises themselves as servants of righteousness (2nd Corinthians 11:15) Lying stems from a much more serious character defect than we might imagine. Evil is described as lies, both in work and deed, in order to create an image pleasing to others and then see themselves the way others see they, thus creating and adopting a phony self-image. If you would live forever in the society of God/Elohim, you are commanded by "Him" who give you life and breath "Wherefore putting away lying, speaking every man truth with his neighbor: for we are members one of another" Eph. 4:25. Men lie because they are more concerned with their own self-esteem and sense of importance than they are with ultimate good of their fellowman. They speak and act falsely because they fear the opinions of men much more than that of "Almighty God Himself"! it is the real truth which will make you free (read) St. John 8:32.

TENTH COMMANDMENT

"Thou shalt not covet thy neighbor's house, thou shalt not covet thy neighbor's wife, nor his manservant, nor his maidservant, nor his ox, nor his ass, nor anything that is thy neighbor's "

Covetousness: An intense desire to possess something (or someone) that belongs to another person (take heed) and beware of covetousness, for one's life does not consist in the things he possesses. Luke 12:15.

This commandment is different from the other (9) commandments for it pertains specifically to the heart.

This act of covetousness occurred initially in the Garden of Eden: Adam and Eve given permission to eat fruit from any of the trees of the garden except one, the "tree of knowledge of good and evil" Gen. 2:16-17. But under the guise of Satan (snake) Eve saw that the tree was good for food, and that it was a delight to both of their eyes, and the tree was to be desired to make one wise and ate and she also gave some to Adam and he ate. Gen. 3:16. Adam and Eve had misdirected desire; which was covetousness or lust.

This forbidden fruit was appealing to their senses. It looked good (delightful to their eyes) undoubtedly and was seen as a means of obtaining wisdom (was to be desired to make one time).

Do not love the world or things in the world if anyone loves the world, the love of the Father is not in him, for all that is in the world. The desire of the flesh and desire of the eyes and pride in possession: is not from the Father, but is from the world and the world is passing away, along with its desires. but whosoever does the will of God/Elohim abides forever. 1ˢᵗ John 2:15-17.

This command regulates even the thoughts in the mind of man and you must learn to obey this commandment; if you are ever able to receive eternal life and glory in the kingdom of God/Eloim!

We are to grow in God/Elohim character during this life; such as Enoch, Noah, Abraham and other servants of the "Most-High" to walk with God We must go "His" way, do as "He does, as he thinks" Blessed are the pure in heart for they shall see God. Matt. 5:8. This scripture is emphasized by "Yahshua the Messiah" indicating of importance of our mind being changed, converted and cleaned up.

This lesson is for God's/Elohim messengers today, to give to who are the people very much in need of knowledge of the character and purpose of the TRUE AND LIVING GOOD!!!

AND IN MY CONCLUSION:

And ye shall know the truth, and the truth shall make you free: St. John 8:32.

Truth is of God/Elohim: deception in all its myriad forms is of Satan, and whoever in any way departs from the straight line of truth is betraying himself unto the power of the wicked one. Those who have learned of the "Messiah" will "have no fellowship with the unfruitful works of darkness" Esp. 5:11. In speech, or as in life they, the simple, the straight forward, and true: for they are preparing for the fellowship of those "holy ones" in whose moth is found no-guide for they are without fault before the throne of God. Rev. 14:15.

According to the teaching of the Holy Scriptures, the only man that will endure is the man whose builder and maker is God/Elohim. With the eyes of faith, man may behold the threshold of heaven, flushed with God's/Elohim's living glory. Through "His" ministering servants (the prophets) the "Lord Jesus Christ" is calling. Upon man to strive with sanctified thoughts/ambition to secure the immortal inheritance "Yahshua the Messiah" urges us to lay up treasure beside his throne of the "Great I Am". Man has endeavored to remove from the prophets the truth from "Yahweh, Himself".

The truth being said by the "the Most-High God" If you love me, keep my commandments. St. John 14:15.

The first (1-4) four commandments are our duty to our Lord, our Savior, "Yahshua the Messiah" and the second (5-10) commandments is our duty to man.

The Commandments of God are not difficult to adhere/abide/live by:
These commandments are for all people (nations) not just for a certain ethnicity
These commandments are for those who truly love the "Omnipotent One"
These commandments are for those who obey, live righteously and upright before "Him"
"Then shall I not be ashamed, when I have respect unto all thy commandments" Psalm 111:6.

Remember "He" says:

"If you love me, keep my commandments"
St. John 14:15

ABOUT THE AUTHOR

As the servant of the "Most-High God" believes that strict observance of the Commandments of God/ Elohim/Yahshua the Messiah, Jesus the Christ is required Exodus 20:1-17, Revelation 22:14, Psalm 111:7-8, James 4:12, Malachi 3:6, Matthew 5:17, John 5:23, and Revelations 14:12.

As the servant of God: emphasizing the observance of the Seventh Day Sabbath (Friday & Saturday) evening, sunset, going down of the sun = (God's time) as a sign between God/Elohim and "His" people as well as God/Elohim's feast days rather than religious days instituted by men. Gen. 2:1-3, Exodus 20:8-11, Ezek. 20:20, Matt. 12:12, Mk. 2:29.

As the servant of God: believing in the "Divine power of God" to heal according to one's faith. James 5:12-15 to receive.

As the servant of God: believe in eating a selected diet, God/Elohim has prepared a menu for the health and welfare of "His" people. Leviticus 11.

As the servant of God: believes in the "New Birth", receiving the "Holy Ghost", speaking in other tongues as the spirit of God/Elohim gives utterance. Matt. 18:3, John 3:3, Acts 2:1-4 and II Corinthians 6:17.

As the servant of God, the "Most-High God/Elohim/Yahshua the Messiah/Jesus the Christ" are one. The father took on the flesh and came in the form of the Son to redeem man from sin, because no one else in heaven or earth was found worthy. Isaiah 9:6, II Tim. 3:16.

As the servant of Elohim: all scriptures are valid. It is not wise or using wisdom to esteem the Old Testament over the New Testament, nor the New Testament over the Old Testament Mal. 3:6. The servant of God believes you must live by the whole book and that they do not contradict one another. Isaiah 40:8, II Timothy 3:16-17, II Peter 1:21, Romans 15:4, Psalms 119:105 and John 17:7.

As the servant of Elohim: baptism in the name of (Yahshua) Jesus is essential and that in doing so, we can indeed baptize in the name of the Father which is God (Elohim) the Son which is God, the Holy Ghost — which is also God. Acts 2:38, Acts 22:16, Acts 10:46-48, Matt. 28:19 and Mk 16:15-16.

As the servant of God: do believe that the Millennium, i.e., the Saints shall dwell with (Yahshua) Jesus a thousand years and shall judge the world. 1ˢᵗ Corinthians 5:2, Rev. 20:4-6.

As the servant of "Yahshua the Messiah/Jesus the Christ":

Am ordained as God's Prophetess
Am ordained as Elohim's Pastor
Am ordained as Yahshua the Messiah's Evangelist
Am ordained as Jesus the Christ's Missionary

As the servant of our Lord (Yahweh): do believe that one day Yahshua (Jesus) will return and the dead in the Messiah (Christ) will be resurrected as incorruptible agents to dwell with our Lord (Yahweh). I Corinthians 15:51-55.

As the servant of "Most-High God": the "Passover" is required to acknowledge that God/Elohim/Yahshua the Messiah (Jesus the Christ) did deliver us from the slave of bondage and did die for our sins as outlined in the Old Testament and the New Testament God our Father, Elohim, the might God, Yahweh our Lord, Yahshua the Messiah (Jesus the Christ) SON OF THE LIVING GOD!!!

The "Passover" had to take place in order for the descending of the "Messiah's death Yah" to Have taken place!!!

For more information, please visit www.understandinggodscommandmentsintodaysworld.com.

www.ingramcontent.com/pod-product-compliance
Lightning Source LLC
Chambersburg PA
CBRC100835110726
48006CB00009B/1406